SEEKING
THE
KINGDOM

Also available in the "How to" series:

Effective Evangelism	Ben Davies
Enjoying God's Grace	Terry Virgo
Growing Up as a Christian	Roger Day
Handling Your Money	John Houghton
Joining the Church	Richard Haydon-Knowell
Knowing God's Will	Phil Rogers
Leading a Housegroup	Richard Haydon-Knowell
Learning to Worship	Phil Rogers
Praying the Lord's Prayer	Terry Virgo
Presenting Jesus in the Open Air	Mike Sprenger

For further information on the "How to" series and New Frontiers International, please write to New Frontiers International, 21-23 Clarendon Villas, Hove, Brighton, East Sussex, BN3 3RE.

How to...
STUDY SERIES

SEEKING THE KINGDOM

JOHN HOSIER

NEW FRONTIERS INTERNATIONAL

WORD PUBLISHING
WORD (UK) Ltd
Milton Keynes, England
WORD AUSTRALIA
Kilsyth, Victoria, Australia
WORD COMMUNICATIONS LTD
Vancouver, B.C., Canada
STRUIK CHRISTIAN BOOKS (PTY) LTD
Maitland, South Africa
ALBY COMMERCIAL ENTERPRISES PTE LTD
Balmoral Road, Singapore
CHRISTIAN MARKETING NEW ZEALAND LTD
Havelock North, New Zealand
JENSCO LTD
Hong Kong
SALVATION BOOK CENTRE
Malaysia

SEEKING THE KINGDOM

ISBN 0-85009-184-5 (Australia 1-86258-104-5)

Unless otherwise indicated, Scripture quotations are from the New
International Version (NIV).
© 1978 New York International Bible Society

The quotations on pages 11 and 14 are taken from *The Kingdom of God*
by John Bright, (Nashville, Abingdon Press, 1953) and used by
permission.

The quotation on pages 51 to 52 is taken from *The Presence of the
Future*, by George Eldon Ladd (SPCK, 1974) and used by permission.

The quotations on pages 61 to 62 and page 73 are taken from *Kingdom Manifesto* by Howard A. Snyder, © 1985 by InterVarsity Christian Fellowship of the U.S.A.. Used by permission of InterVarsity
Press, P.O. Box 1400, Downers Grove, IL 60515, U.S.A..

Typesetting by ALMAC, Northampton and printed and bound in
Great Britain by Cox & Wyman Ltd., Reading.

90 91 92 93 / 10 9 8 7 6 5 4 3 2 1

FOREWORD

The "How to" series has been published with a definite purpose in view. It provides a set of workbooks suitable either for housegroups or individuals who want to study a particular Bible theme in a practical way. The goal is not simply to look up verses and fill in blank spaces on the page, but to fill in gaps in our lives and so increase our fruitfulness and our knowledge of God.

Peter wrote his letters to "stimulate wholesome thinking" (2 Peter 3:1). He required his readers to think as well as read! We hope the training manual approach of this book will have the same effect. *Stop, think, apply* and *act* are key words.

If you are using the book on your own, we suggest you work through the chapters systematically, Bible at your side and pen in hand. If you are doing it as a group activity, it is probably best to do all the initial reading and task work before the group sessions – this gives more time for discussion on key issues which may be raised.

Unless otherwise stated, all quotations from the Bible are from the New International Version which you are, in the main, encouraged to use when you fill in the study material.

Terry Virgo
Series Editor

SPECIAL THANKS

I am very grateful to Mary Austin for all her hard work in listening to recordings of my preaching on this theme and for working through my notes in order to present this book to you in its present form.

NEW FRONTIERS INTERNATIONAL is a team ministry led by Terry Virgo and involved in planting and equipping churches according to New Testament principles with a view to reaching this generation with the gospel of the Kingdom. They are also responsible for a wide range of conferences, training programmes and the production of printed and audio teaching materials.

Contents

Introduction

"You may begin the exam." The invigilator sat down and looked round the room. Papers rustled, then silence reigned. He watched the changing expressions of the Bible College students as they glanced through the questions. Several of the young people caught his eye and sighed deeply before they picked up their pens and began to write.

Sitting by the window in the second row, Jim was chewing the end of his biro and trying to recall what he had been learning over the previous fortnight. He gazed hard at the question:

Jesus said: "Seek first (God's) kingdom" (Matt 6:33).

a) What is the Kingdom of God?

b) How can we seek it first?

Jim stared out of the window for a few seconds. The thought flashed through his mind: "I wonder how many Christians out there understand what the Kingdom is and know how to seek it first." Then, turning back to his exam paper, he started to prepare an outline.

Many of us Christians "out there" would probably not know how to tackle that exam question. We have heard the term, "Kingdom of God" and may be able to give a general idea of what it means. But we might be taken off guard if we were required to speak eloquently on the subject, to respond with exam precision.

Jesus did not tell His disciples, "Seek *casually* (God's) kingdom and his righteousness." For Him, the Kingdom was of paramount importance. "You must seek it first – above everything else," He told them. But how can we do that unless we know what it is?

This book has been designed to answer the two questions already mentioned. It is for those who want to know what the Kingdom is and whose greatest desire is to make it their highest priority. My prayer is that as you read, God will increase your understanding of the Kingdom and give you grace to live for it.

Chapter 1 WHAT IS THE KINGDOM OF GOD?

In one of his books about the Kingdom of God, the theologian John Bright writes, "The concept of the Kingdom of God involves . . . the total message of the Bible." Indeed, some people have even suggested that Jesus Himself was obsessed with the Kingdom. Such comments may be over-statements, but the fact remains that Jesus wants us to be enthusiastic for the Kingdom, He wants us to be taken up with it.

Background to the Kingdom

Some Christians think that the Kingdom of God is solely a New Testament concept. "It comes without warning," they say. "John the Baptist stepped into history and introduced the subject, then Jesus took over from him. Before long, everyone was hearing teaching about the Kingdom."

But the Kingdom of God is not found in the New Testament alone. Glance through any Bible concordance and you will see that it is a recurrent theme all the way through the Old Testament scriptures. Read Psalm 145:10-13 and fill in the gaps:

All you have made will praise you, O Lord. Your saints will extol you.

They will tell of the ....

and speak of your might, so that all men may know of your mighty acts and

the ....

Your .... kingdom, and your dominion

endures through all generations.

The Jews of the Old Testament were far from indifferent towards the Kingdom of God. For centuries, they longed for God to break in with power and establish His Kingdom which, in their understanding, would be a period of great prosperity and success for Israel. This kingdom, they thought, would probably be secured through a military regime.

Time passed and hopes for the promised kingdom waned. Abundance did not come, poverty did. The Assyrians and Babylonians invaded and destroyed the nation. Jerusalem was razed to the ground, the Temple was reduced to rubble and leading Jews were taken into exile in Babylon.

After seventy years of captivity, the Jews returned to their country. They rebuilt Jerusalem and the Temple, but still saw no evidence of the establishment of the Kingdom of God among them. They knew about it – particularly through the prophecies of Daniel who described the Kingdom as a rock which "became a huge mountain and filled the whole earth" (Dan 2:35). The Jews were excited by the prospect of this great manifestation of the kingdom. They longed for it but it never seemed to materialize.

Read Daniel 2:44 and write down what Daniel said would be the characteristics of the Kingdom:

In the time of those kings, the God of heaven will set up a kingdom that will . . .

a) never ....

b) nor ....

c) It will crush ....

d) and bring ....

e) It will endure ....

During the 400 years from Malachi to John the Baptist no prophet was raised up by God to address the Israelite nation. The rabbis, however, constantly taught people to expect God to break in. "When the Kingdom comes . . .," they said, ". . . the voice of the prophet will be heard again, Satan's kingdom will disintegrate and salvation – in the form of great prosperity and harmony – will come to the Jews. Then God will raise up His people to declare the Kingdom, His rule, to other nations."

So, for the Jews, the Kingdom of God was not some new teaching. It was, rather, a hope that was always with them – probably the greatest desire of their hearts.

In the light of this fervour for the Kingdom, it is easy to understand why John the Baptist generated such enthusiasm among the people. Here they

were, under Roman domination, and out there in the desert was a prophet with a message about the imminent arrival of the Kingdom. It is hardly surprising that the crowds flocked to him.
Write out his message:

.... (Matt 3:2)
Note: Matthew commonly uses the term "kingdom of heaven" instead of "kingdom of God".

Jesus began His own ministry by talking of the Kingdom.
Write out His first words which are recorded in Mark's gospel:

....

.... (Mark 1:15)
Jesus' ministry did not centre round some vague, theological concept or a novel new teaching. Like John, He was telling the people that the Kingdom of God was on the doorstep. He was deliberately awakening the Jewish hope for the day of God's intervention.

So later, when Jesus declared, "The stone the builders rejected has become the capstone; the Lord has done this, and it is marvellous in our eyes" (Matt 21:42), the Jews would have known that He was alluding to Daniel's vision. Their ears would have pricked up and their deep longings for the Kingdom would be aroused.

The problem for the Jews was that Jesus did not only arouse their longings, He also provoked their indignation.
Choose the appropriate word in the following list for each gap in the text taken from Matthew 21:43-44:

     stone, given, pieces, falls, away, broken, fruit, people, crushed, taken, produce, falls

"Therefore I tell you that the kingdom of God will be .... from

you and .... to a .... who will .... its

.... He who .... on this .... will be

.... to .... , but he on whom it .... will be

...."

Immediately they heard these words, the Jews wanted to arrest Jesus. Why? Because He was telling them that the Kingdom that they longed for would be ripped out of their hands and given to others. "You are not the subjects of this Kingdom,'' He was saying. ''It will fall on and destroy you.'' No wonder His hearers were enraged!

Definition of the Kingdom

John Bright, the theologian, comments:

''... for all this repeated mention of the Kingdom of God, Jesus never once paused to define it. Nor did any hearer ever interrupt Him to ask, 'Master, what do these words, Kingdom of God, which you use so often, mean?' On the contrary, Jesus used the term as if assured that it would be understood and indeed it was. The Kingdom of God lay within the vocabulary of every Jew. It was something they understood and that they longed for desperately.''

The use of the word ''kingdom'' in the Bible can be very confusing for those of us who live in a country which is sometimes referred to as the United Kingdom. If we are not careful, our understanding of a ''kingdom'' can be coloured by our experience of leadership in our nation.

In the United Kingdom, we have a head of state and elect a separate head of government. The Queen is generally much respected but she has no real governmental authority over the nation. She reigns over our country, but the Prime Minister (with Parliamentary backing) actually rules it. We are seen as subjects of the Queen, but we really live under a government led by a Prime Minister. When you compare this ''kingdom'' with the Bible definition of the term ''kingdom'', the United Kingdom is actually not a kingdom at all.

Both the Hebrew and Greek words for ''kingdom'' refer to the authority and sovereignty exercised by one person, the king. This man inherits his position, so he cannot be voted into office or out of it. Whatever he commands is law and no one can debate or oppose his will. Since his position is inherited, his subjects are his by that inheritance.

So let us answer the question posed at the beginning of this chapter: What is the Kingdom of God?

It is the government of God – His rule and authority on earth which I should like to summarize as:

THE KINGDOM OF GOD IS GOD'S WILL BEING EXPRESSED.

This Kingdom has past, present and future expressions – as we shall see.

Chapter 2 THE KINGDOM IN THE PAST

"The Kingdom of Heaven is near," John the Baptist declared to the people. Then he pointed them to Jesus.

The Kingdom has Come
When Jesus began His ministry, He proclaimed the same message as His forerunner – "The Kingdom of God is near" – but to it He added the words, "The time has come". By this statement He was saying more than John. He was telling His hearers that the Kingdom was wrapped up in Himself. He was closing one age and opening another.

There are four ways in which we can see the Kingdom revealed in the person of Jesus.

i) He reflects the Kingdom in His character
Read John 6:38.

Where did Jesus come from? ....

What didn't He come to do? ....

What did He come to do? ....
Since the Kingdom is the will of God being expressed, Jesus expressed the Kingdom in His character by being dedicated to the will of God. This commitment also emerges in a later statement that He makes. Here is a scrambled version of this statement. Work it out, then write it down and check it in John 8:29.

"He always pleases me; for the One left me has Him who is not sent with me, what I do alone."

....

....

15

....

When Jesus came to earth He was bringing heaven down with Him, expressing the Kingdom, God's will among men – whom He taught to pray, ''Your Kingdom come, your will be done on earth as it is in heaven''.

ii) He confers the authority of the Kingdom
Read Matthew 12:29.

What must you do before you can rob a strong man's house?

....

The Pharisees had just suggested that Jesus had joined forces with the devil and was casting out demons by Satan's power (Matt 12:24). But Jesus was quick to point out that He had not come to ally Himself with Satan but to destroy his works. ''I have the authority to bind the devil so that He can be plundered,'' Jesus was saying. ''He is strong but I am stronger.'' He proved His words by casting out demons.

Not only does Jesus have the authority to bind Satan, He also confers it on Peter and on His church. All Jesus' disciples have the authority to bind the devil.

Correct the following statement:

''I will loan you the keys of the kingdom of heaven; a number of things that you bind on earth may be bound in heaven, and a few things that you loose on earth could be loosed in heaven.''

....

....

....

.... (Matt 16:19)

How do we exercise this binding ministry? I believe that we bind through commanding prayer. When we seek God on major issues we generally discover that we need to persist in prayer for some time before He responds to us. There will, however, be those occasions when God gives us special authority to bind and loose – ''Be healed in Jesus' name!'', ''I command that . . .''. Such prayers manifest God's Kingdom in a very powerful way.

16

iii) He identifies with the Kingdom

Jesus said, "The secret of the kingdom of God has been given to you. But to those on the outside everything is said in parables..." (Mark 4:11). By this He was telling us that there are mysteries in the Kingdom which cannot be understood unless God gives revelation. As Jesus' disciples, we have the privilege of knowing the secrets – one of which concerns Jesus' subtle identification of Himself with the Kingdom.

As we have already seen, Jesus referred to Daniel's vision about the stone that would crush other kingdoms, become a great mountain and fill the earth. The Jews would have known that He was alluding to the coming Kingdom of God but they may not have realized that Jesus was actually telling them, "I am that stone. I identify with the Kingdom. As the Kingdom comes, people are going to be in conflict with me." Later, after Jesus' death and resurrection, Peter made it perfectly clear that: "He (Jesus) is 'the stone you builders rejected, which has become the capstone'." (Acts 4:11)

Fill in the gaps:

Once, having been asked by the Pharisees when the kingdom of God would come, Jesus replied, "The kingdom of God does not come ...., nor will people say, ' .... ' or ' .... ' because the kingdom of God is within (among) you." (Luke 17:20-21)

There is a difficulty here. Jesus is talking to the Pharisees and He would be unlikely to tell them that the Kingdom is "within" them. He may be using general terminology: "The Kingdom does not come visibly in the way that earthly kingdoms often come, with armies, elections etc., because the Kingdom of God is within people." Or Jesus may be saying, "The Kingdom of God is 'in among' you, since wherever I am, there also is the Kingdom – God ruling and expressing His will through me."

iv) He does the works of the Kingdom

Early in His ministry Jesus went into the synagogue in Nazareth, stood up before the people and read from the scriptures. His text was a passage which expressed the rule of God and which was commonly known to refer to the Kingdom.

Read Luke 4:18-19.

Write down how the rule of God would be manifest:

(i) ....

(ii) ....

(iii) ....

(iv) ....

(v) ....

Having read the passage, Jesus returned the scroll to the attendant, sat down and said . . . what?

....

.... (Luke 4:21)

Whether they realized it or not, Jesus was telling His hearers, "The Kingdom has already come and its fulfilment is through me."

John the Baptist, isolated in prison, began having doubts about Jesus' ministry. Had he been mistaken to point out this man as the "Lamb of God"? To find out the truth, he sent some of his disciples to Jesus to ask, "Are you the one who was to come, or should we expect someone else?" (Luke 7:20)

Fill in the missing verbs in Jesus' reply:

"Go back and report to John what you have .... and .... : the blind .... sight, the lame .... , those who have leprosy .... , the deaf .... , the dead .... ,and the good news .... to the poor" (Luke 7:22).

Jesus was telling John, "Isaiah's prophecy applies to me. Look at my ministry and you will see the works of the Kingdom. The rule of God has come through me."

Perhaps the clearest sign that the Kingdom had come lay in a comment that Jesus made after He had been casting out demons. He said, "If I drive out demons by the Spirit of God, then the kingdom of God has come upon you'' (Matt 12:28). Clearly He was identifying the expulsion of demons with the presence of the Kingdom – which is another way of saying, ''God's rule is seen through my ministry.''

So the Kingdom has already come – in a Person. To find out what the rule of God is like, look at the ministry of Jesus. He expressed God's will on earth. If you encounter Jesus, you automatically encounter the Kingdom.

There are ten marks of the rule of God:
1. The poor receive good news.
2. The prisoners hear about freedom.
3. The blind recover their sight.
4. The oppressed are released.
5. The time of God's favour is proclaimed.
6. The lame walk.
7. The lepers are cleansed.
8. The deaf hear.
9. The dead are raised.
10. Demons are expelled.

These things can be summarized under four headings:
A Salvation
B Release
C Healing
D Deliverance

The ministry of Jesus is the rule of God.

The Kingdom of God does not simply have past relevance. It also expresses itself in the present and future.

The Kingdom is Now
Some people have difficulty in bringing together the church and the Kingdom. ''The church equals the Kingdom,'' they say. But this is not absolutely true. The Kingdom of God – God's will being expressed – has a future dimension as well as a present-day application. It is therefore much broader than the church.

Having said that the church does not equal the Kingdom, we must beware that we do not completely separate the two from one another: ''That's the Kingdom over there and here's the church.'' Although the church is not the entire Kingdom of God, the Kingdom – the rule of God – finds its expression through the church. The relationship between them could therefore be illustrated in the following way:

Since the Kingdom is the expression of God's will, and the church is contained within the Kingdom, then the church should naturally be demonstrating the Kingdom.

Jesus likens the Kingdom to a mustard seed which starts small, grows into a big tree and becomes the perching place for many birds (Luke 13:19). This parable, which focuses on the growth of the Kingdom, could equally relate to the church. The church begins with a handful of disciples, spreads throughout the world and demonstrates God's will on the earth.

Sometimes a shop will display a sign which reads: UNDER NEW MANAGEMENT. That same sign should stand over the church. When we become Christians we no longer rule our own lives. They belong to Jesus. He is our King and we are His subjects. Just as you can often tell someone's nationality by looking at him, so you should be able to detect the Kingdom person. He is the one who expresses the will of God.

Jesus was a Kingdom person. He was a man accredited by God to us by . . . what?

.... , ... and .... (Acts 2:22)

These things are evidence to us that . . . what?

....

.... (John 14:11)

If we have faith in Jesus, what will we do?

....

.... (John 14:12)

Wherever Jesus exercises His ministry, God rules. Where God rules, things happen.

It is important for us to note that although Jesus performed many amazing miracles, He could not fully express the Kingdom on earth. He healed many sick people, but they became ill again. He raised Lazarus from the dead, but one day Lazarus died again. He stilled a storm on the Lake of Galilee, but there were more storms after that. Jesus' signs were evidence that the Kingdom had come, God's will was being expressed, but there were limitations. The miracles were signposts to the fullness of the Kingdom which was yet to come.

God is moving in some remarkable ways in today's church. We are seeing God's Kingdom come – people are being set free, healed and delivered. But we are also acutely aware of our limitations. We have to hold in tension the present and the eternal perspectives of the Kingdom. The Kingdom is breaking in now through signs and wonders, nevertheless these things are pointing to a perfect wholeness which is found in heaven.

That is not to say that health and wholeness will come only when we die. Since the church is an expression of God's rule and will, we should be seeing all around us the works of the Kingdom: salvation, release, healing and deliverance. These things will not be perfectly manifest here on earth, but they should be happening because they are signs of the Kingdom and the Kingdom has come in Jesus.

Even when Jesus was on earth, He was limited in His Kingdom works. He had come to fulfil Isaiah's prophecy – which He read in the synagogue at the start of His ministry – but He could not fulfil part of it for John the Baptist. When John's disciples came to check if Jesus really was the one they had been looking for, Jesus pointed to the evidence of His ministry and almost quoted Isaiah 61:1-2. But He missed out two significant elements: freedom for the captives and release for the prisoners.

Bearing in mind John's situation, why do you think this was?

....

....

The message here is that although we cannot receive all the Kingdom in the present age, we should lay hold of as much of it now as we possibly can.

Who lays hold of the Kingdom?

.... (Matt 11:12)

The Kingdom is taken by godly Christians through fervent, commanding, binding prayer and Spirit-inspired activity. Are you one of those people?

The Kingdom is Coming

Jesus taught us to pray, ''Your kingdom come, your will be done on earth as it is in heaven'' (Matt 6:10). He was effectively saying, ''You haven't got all the Kingdom yet. There's a future dimension to it. Pray for the Kingdom to burst in among you in greater fullness than you already know.''

22

The breaking in of the fullness of the Kingdom at the end of the age is marked by three main characteristics.

i) Restoration
Read Acts 3:21.

Jesus is waiting in heaven for something – what?

....

The prophets before Jesus also looked forward to this time. In the later chapters of Isaiah, the prophet spoke a great deal about God's final plan of restoration when the Kingdom of God would come with such power that the whole universe would be transformed by it.

The New Testament also takes up the theme of the restoration of all things.
Read Romans 8:22-23.

What has the whole creation been doing while it waits for restoration?

....

What are we doing while we wait for our adoption?

....

Read Isaiah 51:6 and 2 Peter 3:12.

What will happen to the heavens?

....

....

What will happen to the earth/elements?

....

....

Read Isaiah 65:17 and 2 Peter 3:13.

What will God give us to replace them?

....

This is probably the only teaching in the world that gives an answer to the question: ''What's the point of all the deadness in the vast recesses of space?'' The message of restoration tells us that one day the Kingdom will come in its fullness and the universe will live. One of the great joys for those who belong to the Kingdom will be the freedom to explore the transformed universe through which God will express His Kingdom purposes for ever.

Two of the marks of the Kingdom on earth are the overthrow of evil and release from bondage. When the Kingdom comes in its fullness, these things will happen on a cosmic scale: evil will be totally overthrown and the whole creation will be released from bondage to decay.

ii) Wholeness
It is God's plan to make everything new (Rev 21:5). Along with the new heaven and earth will also come a new wholeness.
Read Revelation 21:4.

What will God do?

....

What four things will not exist any more?

....

Jesus expressed the will of God on earth. He raised the dead, made sad people happy and healed the sick. But all these things recurred again.

When the Kingdom comes in its fullness, the works of Jesus will be perfected. There will be complete wholeness for everyone throughout eternity.

Two more marks of the Kingdom are healing and resurrection. Jesus demonstrated them on earth; they will be fully realized in heaven.

iii) Universal kingship
Although many people do not realise it, Jesus is reigning now. He will continue to rule until God's appointed time.
Read 1 Corinthians 15:24-25.

When the end comes what will Jesus do?

....

What must He destroy before then?

....

Where will His enemies be at that time?

....

When the Kingdom comes in its fullness, everyone everywhere will bow
and confess that Jesus is the King of His Kingdom (Phil 2:10-11). Christ's
righteousness will fill the entire universe. The unredeemed will have to
submit to God's judgement, while the redeemed will rejoice in God's
presence for ever.
Read Revelation 11:15.

What will happen to this world?

....

What will Christ do?

....

Read Revelation 5:13 and write down the words of the song that one day
you will sing as you stand before the throne:

....

Two further marks of the Kingdom are salvation and the Lord's favour.
God's people have these in measure on earth, but when the Kingdom
comes in its fullness we will have perfect everlasting salvation and God's
favour will rest on us for all eternity.

To Summarize
Christians look back to *the Kingdom that has come*. Through His ministry
on earth, Jesus established the Kingdom – the will and rule of God. His
works were evidence that the Kingdom was already among us, in His own
person.
Look up Colossians 1:13 and write down what Jesus has already done for
us (in the past):

....

....

Christians note that *the Kingdom is also in the present*. The church is God's means of expressing His Kingdom. If we do not see signs and wonders accompanying the preaching of the Word, how else will people know that God rules? Although we will not experience perfect wholeness on earth, we must bring in as much of the Kingdom as we can. God has called us to be a Kingdom people; we cannot settle for anything less.

Look up Hebrews 12:28 and write down what we are doing now (in the present):

....

....

Christians look forward to *the Kingdom still to come* – not a static, boring place, but one full of great joy which is just waiting to be explored. It will be God's restored universe – a new heaven and earth where righteousness dwells and where all suffering is banished. That is our future destiny: a permanent home in the presence of the King, enjoying His rule – His Kingdom – for ever.

Look up Matthew 25:34 and write down what we will do one day (in the future):

....

....

Chapter 4 OTHER THEORIES ABOUT THE KINGDOM

Throughout history people have put forward many different ideas about the Kingdom of God. These views, although they have tended to be narrow and insufficient, all contain elements of the truth and are instructive for us. In this chapter we shall consider six different views.

1. The Kingdom is the Church

Way back in church history, Augustine put forward a view that has become dominant in Catholic theology: The Kingdom equals the church. He said that the power of the Kingdom is directly equivalent to the power and authority of the church. Where the church is able to extend its boundaries into mission, there is the direct equivalent of the extension of the Kingdom.

This view was shared by many of those who were involved in the early housechurch movement. ''If the Kingdom equals the church, we must get the church right,'' they thought. This desire was, in a sense, really quite helpful. But in recent years charismatics have come to understand that while the church is an expression of the Kingdom, it is not the sum total of the Kingdom – as we noted in the last chapter.

2. The Kingdom is Spiritual and Invisible

Reacting to the Catholic position were those who held to Reformation teaching. They said, ''God is sovereign and exercises His control through the preaching of the Word and through the ministry of the Holy Spirit.'' They therefore saw the Kingdom as something spiritual which cannot be visibly demonstrated.

The major part of teaching about the Kingdom is found in the gospels – because Jesus' consuming passion is the Kingdom. Many non-charismatic evangelicals do not understand the importance of the Kingdom because they have not been taught much about it. Their children learn from the gospels, but the primary focus for the adults is on the epistles – particularly those of Paul. The epistles contain some teaching on the Kingdom but their greater emphasis is on the grace of God and the way of salvation. Clearly, evangelicals who find themselves in this position need to spend more time in the gospels, see the very visible signs of the Kingdom and come into a new understanding of the burden of Jesus' own ministry.

3. The Kingdom is in the Future

A number of Bible teachers view history in terms of dispensations. In other words, there are various periods of time which have definite differences and barriers between them. Those who follow this teaching, the "Dispensationalists", put the Kingdom entirely into the future. In its most extreme form, the belief is that one day the Jewish nation will be able to live out the Sermon on the Mount and establish the Kingdom.

Some evangelicals would not like to consider themselves Dispensationalists, yet they actually hold a dispensational view. They say that there was an age of spiritual gifts, but maintain that supernatural manifestations died out with the apostles. "That age is past. We're now living in a different dispensation," they say, in effect. What they are doing is denying a present breaking-in of the Kingdom in signs and wonders through the church.

4. The Kingdom is Established through Violent Revolution

In recent years we have seen the emergence of something called "Liberation Theology". It has been particularly prevalent in places like Latin American countries which are under oppressive military regimes. Its propagators emphasize the need for violent revolution to promote justice in these nations. They would take up Kingdom statements like the opening of prison doors and assert, "Justice is a mark of God's Kingdom, but if Christians want to see justice done and political prisoners released, they may have to use force."

By considering the political situations of these people, we may well understand how they feel. We cannot, however, condone what they teach. Certainly the Kingdom of God is revolution, because it turns people's lives upside-down. Yet it takes place not through outward physical violence but by the deep inner work of the Holy Spirit.

28

5. The Kingdom is Evolving

This view suggests that there is going to be an evolutionary process which will usher in a golden age and thereby establish the Kingdom of God. It will happen largely through social action, better technology, scientific advance, improved education and so on.

The teaching was popular in the last century and in the early 1900s. Since then we have had two world wars which have somewhat tarnished the idea that we are moving steadily into a golden age. Moreover, the Bible does not say that the Kingdom evolves gradually; it says that the Kingdom bursts in with great immediacy.

6. The Kingdom is Christ Reigning in Me

Some people are very subjective about the Kingdom of God. "The Kingdom is Christ reigning in my life," they say. This may be a true statement – God will express His Kingdom as Jesus reigns in me. But it is also a narrow viewpoint, since Christ will reign *whether I respond to Him or not*. The Kingdom must be seen in much wider terms than simply Christ reigning in me.

So, to recap, the Kingdom is God's rule being expressed and that is not so much a place as a condition. At this very moment, God is ruling, fulfilling His will through His people and bringing something of heaven to earth.

Chapter 5 THE GOSPEL OF THE KINGDOM I

When will the end of the ages come? The answer to this question lies primarily in one verse of scripture.
Read Matthew 24:14 and answer the above question.

....

....

In the past, many of us became excited when we heard that there had been a succession of wars, famines or earthquakes because we thought that the end was close. But if we study scripture faithfully, we will realize that these signs do not actually tell us that the end is on the doorstep.
Fill in the gaps, from Matthew 24:6-8:

"You will hear of .... and ...., but

see to it that you are .... Such

things, ... , but the end is ....

.... will .... against

..............................., and .... against .... There

will be .... and .... in various places.

.... are the .... of ....

...."

Jesus tells us that natural disasters are not reserved for the very end but will continue through all the ages. So three consecutive earthquakes are not the sign that the Second Coming may be about to happen. The end will come only when the gospel has been proclaimed throughout the nations.

There are two other verses in scripture which tell us how we can be involved in the return of the King. The first of these is in the Lord's Prayer. When we pray, ''Your Kingdom come, your will be done on earth as it is in heaven,'' we are asking God to establish His Kingdom both now and in its fullness in the future. Then, secondly, the Bible tells us that by our ''holy and godly lives'' we can actually speed the day of Jesus' return and the fullness of the Kingdom (2 Peter 3:11-12).

Before the end comes, our overriding commission is, as we have already noted, to preach the gospel of the Kingdom to the whole world. Since the Kingdom has past, present and future manifestations, these three elements should be present when we preach the gospel. We need to share with people what God has already done, what He is doing and what He plans to do. This is how Paul proclaimed the gospel of the Kingdom.

Read Romans 15:18-19 and fill in the gaps:

I will not venture to speak of anything except what Christ has accomplished through me in ....

by what I have .... and ....

by the .... , through the

.... So from ....

.... ,

I have .... the ....

Paul accomplished the commission. He went to the nations as he could reach them in his day and proclaimed a complete ''gospel of the Kingdom''. How did he do this? Through his words, through his actions and through signs and miracles – all done through the power of the Holy Spirit.

This sort of proclamation of the gospel is a far cry from much of *our* evangelism. Many of us have been brought up to believe that the gospel message is ''words alone'' and have despised works as ''social gospel'' and wonders as ''counterfeit gospel''.

But the scriptures state that a full proclamation of the gospel involves words, works and wonders – through the power of the Holy Spirit. Paul declared, ''I have fully proclaimed the gospel of Christ'' – so must we.

The word "gospel" means "good news", so the gospel of the Kingdom refers to the good news of the Kingdom. Our mission is to proclaim the reign and rule of God through *words*, *works* and *wonders*, as Paul did. In this chapter we shall consider how to proclaim the gospel through words, and we shall deal with works and wonders in Chapter 6.

Words

Negative words

God wants us to be witnesses with our mouths. Since we have something positive to offer the world, we must speak negatively about what the world has to offer us. The target for our attack is sin – both in general and specific terms.

About a hundred years ago, the evangelist and author R.A. Torrey suggested that the words in Romans 1:26-27 were so shocking that they should not be read out to mixed congregations. People would have been too offended then, but today the story is very different. We can become so familiar with perversions in society that we fail to put an accurate label on sin.

Read Romans 1:26-27 and correct the words which are not right:

Because of this, God was happy for them to experiment with more

interesting love-making. So their women exchanged dull relations for

more exciting ones. In the same way the men also abandoned boring

relations with women and were inspired to love one another. Men enjoyed

wholesome acts with other men, and received in themselves a really good

feeling about their actions.

One Christian leader was so incensed by the teaching in schools about homosexual practices that he read Romans 1 to some councillors in South London. Then he and some church members distributed leaflets in the area telling parents what their children were learning.

We hear about homosexual communities and even homosexual churches. Unmarried couples live together openly. They even have children – yet few people are prepared to say that their conduct is wrong. Sin is fashionable, acceptable. Anyone who dares to confront it will face backlash.

God is relying on us to confront it. These practices are evil. We must address them specifically. We must speak negatively against sin because we have something positive to offer – the gospel of the Kingdom, the reign and rule of God.

Challenging words

Jesus rules as King. When we tell people about Him, we are not simply proclaiming a Saviour who forgives sins. We are not saying, ''Make Jesus your Lord'' – because Jesus is already Lord. We are challenging our hearers to accept a total change of government in their lives.

Read Colossians 2:6 and correct the two mistakes in the version below:

Just as you made Christ Jesus your Lord, continue to live in Him.

A full preaching of the gospel will teach repentance from sin, faith towards Jesus Christ, baptism in water and in the Spirit, and allegiance to the church. People's attitude towards a change of government in their lives is often tested by their attitude to water baptism.

Read Acts 8:36 and tick the right answer below:

When the Ethiopian eunuch received the gospel his first desire was

    to read the 2nd lesson at church on Sunday.

    to join the commitment course.

    to go off and have lunch.

    to be baptized.

This man had experienced a change of government. He did not have to be coaxed into the water. He wanted to demonstrate that Jesus was now Saviour, Lord and ruler of his life.

33

Bearing in mind the story of the eunuch, answer the following questions:

Should believers be baptized?   YES/NO

If YES, when? ....

Have you been baptized?   YES/NO

If NO, give reasons for your answer:

....

....

....

Exciting words

When we talk about Jesus we must communicate excitement. Too many people view Christianity as adherence to a list of do's and don'ts. But following Jesus should be an adventure! The early disciples discovered that. They wanted to be with Jesus because amazing things happened when He was around. His rule generates excitement, so let's be positive as we bring in that rule and excite people when we share Kingdom teaching with them.

Spirit-inspired words

Paul's preaching of the gospel was ''in the power of the Holy Spirit''. We need Holy Spirit power behind our words.

Strangely enough, there is very little in the Bible about praying for people's conversion and quite a lot about praying for the preaching of the gospel.

Fill in the gaps:

Brothers, my .... and ....

to God for the Israelites is that they ....

.... (Rom 10:1)

.... , that whenever I ....

34

.... , ... may be given me so that
I will .... make known the .... of
the .... (Eph 6:19)

So, according to the scriptures, we should pray for conversions but especially for the preaching of the gospel. We should focus not so much on the harvest, as ask God for labourers to be sent into it.

Robert Murray McCheyne was someone who preached in the power of the Holy Spirit. He was born in the last century, had a seven-year ministry, died at the age of twenty-nine but saw a great revival take place in his church. When I read through his sermons I discovered that they were nearly all evangelistic and also, in my estimation, that they were all rather ordinary. It brought home to me very forcefully that we cannot rely simply on words to communicate the message.

Read 1 Thessalonians 1:5.

How did the gospel come to the Thessalonians?

a) with ....

b) with ....

c) with ....

d) with ....

If we are going to preach effectively to the nations, the power of the Holy Spirit must be the motivating force behind everything that we say.

Pray that God will give you the opportunity to tell an unbeliever about Jesus this week.

Chapter 6 THE GOSPEL OF THE KINGDOM II

Paul proclaimed the gospel with words, as we saw in the last chapter. He also proclaimed it through works and wonders.

Works

Justice for the poor is a constant theme of the Bible. Perhaps the best of the many illustrations of this appears in Isaiah 58:6-9.

Read verses 6 and 7.

What are the five main examples of "fasting" here?

1. ....

2. ....

3. ....

4. ....

5. ....

Read verses 8 and 9.

What five main blessings await those who exercise justice?

1. ....

2. ....

3. ....

4. ....

5. ....

Justice for the poor is not just a matter of compassionate concern. It is at the heart of God's Kingdom. The Psalmist declares, "The Lord is King for ever and ever" (Psalm 10:16a), then he goes on to state the implications of the Lord's Kingship and His Kingdom.

Read Psalm 10:16-18.

Who will perish from His land?

....

What does he hear?

....

What does he do?

....

Whom does he defend?

....

For what reason?

....

Part of God's Kingship is justice for the poor. So when Jesus came to manifest the Kingdom in person, He identified with this Old Testament theme and proclaimed good news for the poor. He demonstrated His concern by releasing those who were oppressed or powerless.

Seeking the Kingdom therefore includes a concern for the poor. There are many people around us who are suffering oppression and who are powerless to help themselves. When He was on earth, Jesus acted on their behalf; while we are on earth, we must do the same.

At this point there may be a voice of protest which declares, "Surely, Jesus helped those who were *spiritually* poor." Certainly this is true of everyone outside Christ. But the gospel of the Kingdom is not proclaimed in words alone. Paul was eager to remember the poor (Gal 2:10) and that was not just a mental activity, nor was it confined to such things as door-to-door evangelism. Not everyone is gifted in standing on doorsteps and talking to people about God. Rather than force these people to do this, we

37

would do better to encourage them to find some other more practical way to share the love of Jesus.

Let me suggest some ways in which we can work for the poor.

a) The financially poor

Read Acts 4:33-35.

What did the believers do?

....

....

What did the apostles do?

....

....

Clearly, the early church was a shining witness not just to the power but also to the love of God! Later, Paul commended the Macedonians for their incredible generosity even though they were themselves facing extreme poverty (2 Cor 8:1-4).

Read 2 Corinthians 8:13.

What didn't Paul want?

....

....

What did he want?

....

God does not want His church to be a sort of communistic clique, but He does want to see balance. We often separate England into two nations: north and south, but we dare not divide the church in the same way: the rich and the poor. In the same local church there cannot be Christians who have an abundance of material possessions living contentedly alongside those who can hardly make ends meet.

The world is watching us. Is there equality in our local church? Are we proving by our love that we are Jesus' disciples (John 13:35)? Love gives to poor people. It's Kingdom lifestyle.

Think of someone in your local church who is in financial need. Are you able, out of your abundance, to give him/her some money?

b) The situationally poor

Some people put evangelism and babysitting into two separate categories but they are equally valid. There are many single parents who are poor in the sense that they have been rendered powerless by their situations. From time to time they want to get out in the evenings, but they can do so only if they find someone who is willing to babysit. Such help may seem to us rather menial but God has built concern for others into His Kingdom.

Work out the following:

earthon noe ot dink dan sconeamopatsi eb

.... (Eph 4:32)

List some other practical things that you in particular could do for other people (e.g. mow the lawn):

....

....

....

....

....

Find out if anyone in your local church has a practical need and consider how to meet it.

Could you meet it?   YES/NO

c) The socially poor

Some Christians may feel that God is leading them into full-time work in social action – possibly as AIDS counsellors or workers among those who are trying to give up drugs or considering abortion. Christians in America have set up several crisis pregnancy centres and have seen some amazing results. Of three thousand women who went to one of these centres for counselling, seventy per cent decided not to have an abortion and many were converted and added to the church. Here is a clear example of how the works of the Kingdom produce fruit for the Kingdom.

When we consider being involved in more specialized areas of social action we must be sure that we are acting through the power of the Holy Spirit. God may not want our church to be involved in AIDS counselling, with drug addicts or in crisis pregnancy centres. We can only be sure of His will if we wait for the Spirit to guide us.

Pause for a moment and pray for Christians who are working full-time in social action.

So the gospel of the Kingdom can be proclaimed in words and through works. Some believers do not feel able to speak as freely as they can act. But their practical deeds create the opportunity for relaxed conversation about Jesus. Words and works are therefore both an important part of Kingdom evangelism.

Wonders

Just as words and works will have evangelistic impact, so too will signs and wonders. These demonstrate visibly and forcefully the breaking in of the rule of God.

At one point in Jesus' ministry we read, ''When they heard all (Jesus) was doing, many people came to him . . .'' (Mark 3:8). The crowds did not flock to Jesus because of what He said, but because of what He did.

Read John 12:17-19.

Why did many people go out to meet Jesus?

....

If you hear that someone has preached a wonderful sermon, you might be tempted to go and listen to him. But if you learn that this individual has raised a dead man, you will immediately race off to see him.

Even Jesus' enemies recognised that by raising Lazarus, Jesus had performed an amazing miracle and commented that the world had gone after Him.

Signs and wonders pave the way for the preaching of the gospel.

Fill in the gaps from Acts 8:6:

When the crowds .... Philip and .... the

.... he did, they all ....

.... to what ....

I once knew a retired minister who had been a very powerful evangelist. Before he died he showed me several scrap books of newspaper cuttings about his evangelistic campaigns. One of these campaigns had been in South Wales and had resulted in the conversion of a burly boxer. Underneath the picture of this man the minister had written the words, ''This was my Lazarus''.

When I asked him what this meant he told me that when he was training for evangelistic ministry the principal of his Bible College had said, ''Before you conduct an evangelistic campaign, ask God for a Lazarus. Seek one dramatic conversion because if something really amazing happens, you'll have no problems communicating to the crowds.'' The boxer in South Wales was known for being a notorious character. But when he was soundly converted, the minister had the people coming in large numbers to hear the gospel.

While it is true that wonders capture people's attention, let us not assume that we can always guarantee their conversion. The Pharisees acknowledged that Jesus had performed a miracle but they did not join the crowds and follow Him.

An elderly lady in a church I was pastoring asked me if I would pray for her because she was gradually losing her sight. I gathered the elders and we prayed – without much faith – that God would arrest the disease in her eyes. When she returned to the hospital she was told that a miracle had occurred and that her eyes were all right.

Shortly after this, she met a lady whose son was ill. She had taken him to several hospitals but none of them could explain the reason for his problem – rapid weight loss. The elderly lady told the mother, ''Our pastor will pray for him!'' The two of them came to my study one night and the elders and I prayed for him. From that moment on, his weight increased and he was soon perfectly well again.

I should like to say that the whole family were converted, but they were not. They saw our compassion and the healing opened a door for us to share the gospel with them, but they did not become Christians then. Maybe they will believe at a future date. At any rate, I saw a principle being worked out – that if people see a sign, they will listen to the gospel.

Read Matthew 11:20.

Which cities did Jesus denounce?

....

....

Why did He denounce them?

....

Sometimes Jesus used signs and wonders to demonstrate the way of the Kingdom and to provoke repentance and faith. Jesus condemns Korazin, Bethsaida and Capernaum because they did not repent at His miracles. Apparently even the Sodomites would have done that.

Pray that God will use you to perform wonders for His glory and make up your mind that you will launch out in this way whenever you have the opportunity.

To Summarize
If we want to have Jesus' impact, we must use His methods. The gospel of the Kingdom involves words, works and wonders. It needs to be expressed because only when it has gone out to all nations will the end come.

God has commissioned every one of us with that task – to take the Kingdom wherever He sends us. One day, towards the end of our ministry, He wants to hear a hint of Paul's words on our lips – "I have fully proclaimed the gospel of Christ" (Rom 15:19).

Chapter 7 KINGDOM LIFESTYLE

God wants His rule to be expressed on the earth. He has commissioned His people to do that. We demonstrate His rule by our lifestyle.

Read 2 Peter 3:11-12.

While we wait for Jesus' return, what sort of lives should we live?

....

If you ask some believers what that means, they might suggest more prayer and Bible study. Certainly we need to do these things, but here the question is not, ''What sort of things should we do?'' The emphasis is not on *doing* but on *being*. There is a Kingdom lifestyle specially fashioned for Christians.

God's desire to have a people who would express His rule and will was not a New Covenant idea. It is clear from the Old Testament scriptures that He wanted the Israelites to express His rule by living according to His laws. They, however, refused to adopt His lifestyle and instead allowed themselves to be led into sin by their own stubbornness and by the nations around them.

No matter how much God's people have disappointed Him, God has always persisted with them. When Jesus came to earth He gave us the supreme example of Kingdom lifestyle to imitate. He has given us His Spirit to help us and watches to see how we are getting on.

Fill in the gaps from Titus 2:14:

(Jesus Christ) gave Himself for us to ....

.... and to ....

.... a .... that are ....

.... , ... to do ....

43

Read 1 Peter 2:9-10.

How are we described?

a ....

a ....

a ....

a ....

What are we called to declare?

....

What has God done for us?

....

....

What were we not?   What are we now?

....

What hadn't we received?   What have we received now?

....

As British Christians we are often weak in our understanding of our
peoplehood – probably because we are weak about our sense of nation-
hood. The Americans do not seem to suffer with this problem! They are
proud to be American. The Jews too seem to be a distinctive people with
a very strong sense of identity. We, on the other hand, tend to be cynical
about our nationality and sometimes even think that national pride should
be despised. Sadly, we can let these feelings run over into the church. We
end up with a poor grasp of what it means to be a nation whom God has
chosen to be an expression of His rule and will.

In this connection, there are two scriptures in the New Testament which
state specifically what the Kingdom is. They are Romans 14:17 and 1
Corinthians 4:20. We shall look at the first of these now and the other in
Chapter 10.

Rules and Regulations?

Read Romans 14:17.

The Kingdom is not a matter of – what?

....

It is instead – what?

....

If we take this verse out of context, we will interpret the Kingdom wrongly. We will think that it is not about life's pleasures but about very spiritual issues. In its context, however, this verse is not saying that. Paul is actually telling us that the Kingdom is not a meat and drink religion – "You can eat or drink this but not that". The whole thrust of Romans 14 concerns a "rules and regulations" understanding of Christianity.

People can have a perverted view of Christianity. They create Christian rules for what is right and wrong. "Beethoven is Christian," they say, "and you can buy the Telegraph, vote for the Liberal Democrats, believe in unilateralism and hold hands with your boyfriend or girlfriend. But jazz is not Christian, you mustn't buy the Sun, vote for the Labour Party, believe in nuclear defence or kiss your boyfriend or girlfriend."

List some other "Christian rules".

....

....

....

....

The problem is that once you establish rules like this, you have to find an ever-increasing number of definitions of the rules to cover misdemeanours. This is exactly what happened with the Scribes and Pharisees. They had a law which said that they should not work on the Sabbath, but what constituted work? To cover themselves, they had about forty definitions of work. So when Jesus' disciples were picking and eating corn on the Sabbath they were, according to the Jewish leaders, breaking the law because they were reaping and threshing.

45

Understandably, once you bring in these secondary rules, people become very adept at getting round them! The Scribes and Pharisees said that you were working on the Sabbath if you travelled more than one mile from your home. So if a Jew needed to go two miles on the Sabbath, he would take a cushion with him. When he had walked a mile, he would put the cushion down and it would count as his home. He could then walk the other mile.

When I was teaching in a Bible College, the staff used to have endless discussions about rules and regulations. Should male and female students be allowed in one another's corridors or rooms – even to deliver a telephone message? On this subject it was decided that the student could deliver the message to the room but could not stay there or in the corridor. So we ended up with, say, a male student trying to keep the spirit of the law by lying on the floor with his feet in his own corridor and the rest of him in the female corridor! One male student, who wanted to visit his sick girlfriend, actually climbed a ladder to her first-floor bedroom and chatted through the window!

"No," Paul is saying. "The Kingdom of God isn't like this. It's not a "rules and regulations" religion. It's about righteousness, peace and joy in the Holy Spirit." If your life lacks these characteristics, then it is less than Kingdom lifestyle.

In the past, we may have viewed righteousness, peace and joy in a rather negative manner. I used to think that one of the most powerful ways you could witness was to say "No" when the raffle tickets came round the office! This was something of an embarrassment to me because my mother-in-law used to supply me with shirts from raffles that she had won!

But the Kingdom is not described in negative terms. Paul says that the Kingdom is righteousness, peace and joy in the Holy Spirit. You can't get much more positive than that.

Chapter 8 RIGHTEOUSNESS, PEACE AND JOY

God wants us to express Kingdom rule in our lives – righteousness, peace and joy in the Holy Spirit. Let's take each of these in turn.

Righteousness

We read that "righteousness will be the sceptre of (God's) Kingdom" (Heb 1:8). Righteousness has to do with being right.

Work out the following:

for God who had no sin made us so that we might become sin in Him, to Him be the righteousness of God

....

....

.... (2 Cor 5:21)

This verse highlights the divine exchange that took place at Calvary. Martin Luther once said that Jesus was made the greatest sinner of all. That comment may shock us, but sometimes we need to be shaken out of our indifference to the familiar. 2 Corinthians 5:21 is itself an amazing statement – God made Jesus sin for us. He clothed Jesus in our sin, and us in Jesus' righteousness.

Many Christians need the courage to accept that what the Bible says about them is true. Some believers think that it is wrong not to be regarded as sinful, wrong to say, "I'm righteous", and wrong not to feel at least a little bit guilty! But if God's word disputes all these suppositions, who are we to challenge it?

Correct the two words which are wrong in the following:

Count yourselves guilty of sin but alive to God in Christ Jesus. (Rom 6:11)

"But," you argue, "you're advocating sinless perfection. I know I'm a sinner. Just look at all the things I do wrong." That's where you are mistaken. The Bible says that as new creations we no longer have a sinful nature. We are 100% righteous in Christ. We must now do what the word tells us: count ourselves dead to sin and live from our new nature – righteousness. We can still sin – by choice, but we can also choose not to sin.

Read Romans 6:12.

What are we told not to do?

....

Read Romans 6:13.

Give examples of sinful things we can do with our bodies:

overeat, ...

....

....

....

Give examples of righteous things we can do with our bodies:

encourage, ...

....

....

....

The word of God says that we have been justified through faith (Rom 5:1). Many of us have heard justification explained in terms of: "just-as-if-I'd-never-sinned". There is also a legal force behind the word. In His supreme court, God has declared His innocent Son guilty and condemned Him. And He has acquitted sinful people and declared them not guilty.

Correct the mistake in the following statement:

By one sacrifice (Jesus) has made happy for ever those who are being made holy. (Heb 10:14)

The corrected verse is a tremendous statement for all Christians. God looks on you, sees you in His Son and says, "You're perfect for ever!" The paradox is that, because you are currently in the flesh, you will also grow towards perfection.

The Kingdom teaching is that since we are now righteous before God we must be true to our new nature and live righteously. To illustrate this, there is a legal document which says that I am a husband, but it is up to me to *live* like a husband. In the same way, God has made a legal statement about you which says that you are righteous, but it is your responsibility to live righteously. When you live uprightly, you will be expressing the will of God and a Kingdom lifestyle.

Peace

Not only does Romans 5:1 tell us that we are justified through faith, it also says that we have – what?

....

This is also a legal term. We were once enemies of God. He was angry with us because of our sin. Then Jesus stepped in, turned God's wrath away from us and made us His friends. Wherever God's will is expressed there is peace, and where His government increases there is even more peace. That's because good government always produces peace.

Fill in the gaps from Isaiah 9:7:

Of the .... of His .... and

.... there will be ....

All Christians have peace with God but some do not *feel* a sense of peace because they have sinned. Marriage is a permanent relationship, but if the husband and wife have an argument, they can be legally together but emotionally very much apart. They restore their relationship by apologising. In the same way, when we have sinned against God and lost our sense of peace, we will feel close to Him again only when we have repented. For as long as we live at peace with God and one another we will demonstrate Kingdom lifestyle.

Let us never forget that there is a difference between *peace with God* and *the peace of God*. Christians may not feel peaceful but legally they still have *peace with God* through Jesus' death on the cross. They may have lost *the peace of God* because they are not living according to Kingdom principles.

From memory, try to correct this statement:
Be anxious about everything, and in everything, by panic and apprehension, with grumbling, present your gripes to others. And the pieces of rumour, which transpire with undermining, will grate in your hearts and your minds in culpable guilt.

....

....

....

....

....

....

....

Now check your version against Philippians 4:6-7.

From time to time we face pressures: a gas bill that we can't pay or a relationship that needs sorting out. Such things can make us anxious and cause us to lose the peace of God. The Bible tells us not to worry but to be thankful and prayerful. So we praise God that He has met all previous gas bills, or helped us in other relationships, and we ask Him to step in again. If we really pray in faith, anxiety will disperse and God's overwhelming peace will replace it. We will then baffle those whose worldly understanding tells them, ''There's no way he can pay that bill'' or ''She'll never sort out that relationship''.

People who live peacefully while under pressure make a great impact because they are not reacting normally. They have adopted a Kingdom lifestyle and are therefore expressing the King's will – peace in every situation regardless of how dreadful it is. To the outsider, that's impressive.

Joy
C.H. Spurgeon, the great preacher, is reported to have said, "Peace is joy resting and joy is peace dancing."

The relationship between joy and happiness is often misunderstood. Some people say that joy is deep and inward while happiness is light and outward. But such a definition creates problems. If I'm dancing with joy in my heart, what does that mean?

The true relationship between joy and happiness is this: joy is unaffected by circumstances while happiness is dependent on circumstances.

"What is joy?" someone once asked me. "Some Christians talk in serious tones about a deep inward joy. Is it like that? The apostle Peter said something about it didn't he?"

How did he describe this joy in 1 Peter 1:8?

....

By this, Peter was not saying, "You can't express this joy." He was saying, "It's so wonderful that you feel that there's a depth you can never fully attain." Those who are outwardly most joyful are not necessarily extroverts, they are people who know inner peace with God. They are joyful because they have discovered that joy is part of the Kingdom lifestyle.

Kingdom joy is not deeply serious, it's exciting. That's why the New Testament expresses it in imagery related to big celebrations. We can see how often in his teaching Jesus would use an illustration of a feast or of a banquet to describe the coming age of the Kingdom of God in its fullness. Eldon Ladd said:

> "So typical of Jesus' ministry was this joyous fellowship that his critics accused him of being a glutton and a drunkard (Matt 11:19). The same note of messianic joy is heard in Jesus' answer to the criticism that he and his disciples did not follow the example of the Pharisees in fasting. Fasting does not belong to the time of a wedding. The presence of the bridegroom calls for joy, not fasting (Mark 2:18-19). While we have no evidence that the metaphor of a bridegroom was applied to the Messiah in Judaism, the wedding

51

feast was a symbol of the Kingdom of God. During the seven days of the wedding festivities, the friends and guests of the bridegroom were excused from the observance of many serious religious duties that they might share in the festivities. Jesus described his presence in the midst of his disciples by this messianic symbol of the wedding. The day of salvation has come, the wedding songs resound; there is no place for mourning, only for joy."

Read Mark 2:18-20.

What were John's disciples doing?

....

Why weren't Jesus' disciples doing the same?

....

By using this picture, Jesus was saying, "The Kingdom of God is wrapped up in me. While I'm actually standing in front of you on earth it's a time not for fasting but for feasting!"

When one day we stand in front of Jesus in heaven, we will not be fasting. We will be shouting, rejoicing, praising, worshipping and feasting at a magnificent wedding celebration. The Father wants the fullness of His Kingdom to be accompanied by great joy.

Read Revelation 19:6-7 and fill in the gaps:

Then I heard what sounded like a .... ,

like the .... of ....

and like .... , ...:

" .... ! For our Lord God Almighty reigns.

Let us .... and .... and give

him .... ! For the .... of the Lamb

has come, and His .... has made herself ready.''

Whenever the Kingdom breaks in, there's joy. It's a joy which should remain unaffected by adverse circumstances. Peter wrote to believers who were facing persecution, yet who were filled with – what?

.... (1 Pet 1:8)

When Paul and Silas were beaten and thrown into jail for preaching the gospel, they did not react like normal prisoners. Sitting in the inner cell with their feet in the stocks they prayed and sang hymns to God! They knew that they had come under the rule of God. They had Kingdom joy – and they were going to express it!

How do you feel about rejoicing in adversity?

....

....

....

....

Are you currently facing difficult circumstances?   YES/NO
How are you reacting to them?

....

....

So the Kingdom is not a meat and drink religion. It is not about rules and regulations, about dressing up unspiritual things to make them look spiritual. That's called legalism. The Kingdom is about righteousness, peace and joy in the Holy Spirit.

God wants all His people to live the Kingdom lifestyle, to express His will. You can discern the people who are doing this by their righteousness, peace and joy. Consider your own life for a moment. Are you one of them?

Chapter 9 KINGDOM LIFESTYLE IN PRACTICE

The question at the end of the last chapter may be difficult to answer. How can we know if we are living righteously, peacefully and joyfully? Clearly we need to have a practical example of Kingdom lifestyle because only then can we measure ourselves against it.

I could give many examples to illustrate Kingdom lifestyle, but one which is always relevant concerns our use of money. That's because the Bible says a great deal about it, and we probably handle it nearly every day.

Over the years, there have emerged two extreme positions in the church regarding the handling of money.

On the one hand, you have Francis of Assisi who would not touch it and who disavowed all his possessions. As his organization expanded and needed to own property, he became furiously angry with his brotherhood for drifting away from his ascetic values.

But on the other hand, you have the ''prosperity preachers,'' some of whom live in the most unbelievable luxury. When they appear – sometimes on American television – they are often in tears, pleading with their viewers to send money to keep the programme going. The dollars pour in, outsiders gain the impression that the whole thing is one big scandal and the reputation of the church plummets.

In England the church is often seen in a bad light where money is concerned. Hoardings outside church buildings display the need of the moment, ''We require £40,000 to restore our church steeple.'' Alongside this sign is a large thermometer which is divided into £1000 sections. As the money arrives, these sections are coloured in and passers-by can see how close the members are to their target.

People who do not belong to the church have approached me and said, ''Your church will probably be holding a jumble sale soon. I have some bits and pieces at home that you might like.'' Outsiders always seem to be under the impression that we run the church on other people's rubbish!

Even door-to-door collectors for so-called Christian organizations are often not believers, and the money they collect does not go to believers either. Certainly justice for the poor is a mark of the Kingdom – as we have already seen. The problem is that outsiders consistently see the church as an institution which scrounges money from the world in order to stay alive.

If we are living a Kingdom lifestyle, we will handle our money with righteousness, peace and joy.

Righteousness
Why do we pay taxes to the governing authorities?

.... (Rom 13:6)
"Give everyone what you owe him" (Rom 13:7).
Give some examples of what you in particular should pay (e.g. TV licence, gas bill)

....

....

....

....

What four specific debts should we pay?

.... (Rom 13:7)
One of the greatest temptations to cheat lies in the area of taxes and revenue. When we fill in our tax return inaccurately, we are not living according to Kingdom principles. Cheating is unrighteous and by failing to submit to the government of our country, we are living unrighteously.

Correct Jesus' words:

"Withhold from Caesar what should be Caesar's."

....

.... (Matt 22:21)
We may object to certain points of government policy, but there is still good reason to pay tax and revenue. The money which is accumulated goes towards education, welfare and other benefits in our nation. We demon-

strate righteous living by honouring the government and giving whatever we owe.

If there is unrighteousness in your financial affairs (e.g. earnings not declared on your tax return, or outstanding debts) make a note of them here:

....

....

....

....

If you are not in the process of sorting it out, take action to do so – or seek help if your financial problems are serious.

Peace

The world is not at peace about money. A member of the wealthy Rockefeller family was asked, ''How much money does a person need to make him happy?'' to which he replied, ''Just a little bit more.'' That's so true! Regardless of how much money we have, we always want more.

Christians do not need to join the world in its anxiety about money. We can be totally at peace because God has told us – what?

....

.... (Heb 13:5)

Our response to this should not be:
''My income will support me; I will therefore not be afraid. What can man do to me?''

Our response is rather – what?

....

.... (Heb 13:6)

We are exhorted, ''Keep your lives free from the love of money and be content with what you have'' (Heb 13:5). If we love money, then peace will turn to striving, and if we are anxious about money, then contentment will turn to jealousy.

How do we cure jealousy? We see someone who apparently has enough money to live comfortably when we are struggling to make ends meet. How can we overcome the jealousy and craving for the income and possessions that this other person enjoys?

When we are jealous of another person, we usually want just *a part* of his life. We do not think of all the things about him that we would not want to have – his ill health, unruly daughter, handicapped son, unbelieving wife, incredibly demanding job. So whenever we are tempted to be jealous of someone, we should look at his whole life and question, ''Would I really want to take on everything he's got?'' Our tendency towards jealousy will probably be lessened when we understand the complete picture.

God promises that He will take care of us and wants us to trust Him – particularly when we are experiencing financial difficulties. As we believe His word, we will experience a great peace.

Correct the following statement:
My God might meet all your needs according to how much He happens to have available at the time.

....

.... (Phil 4:19)

Joy
If righteousness is about our use of money and peace is about our *attitude* towards money, then joy is about our giving money away.

Read 2 Corinthians 9:7.

What should we give?

....

In what two ways should we not give?

....

What does God love?

....

The Greek word translated as "cheerful" is "hilarion" from which we obtain the word hilarious. Clearly God wants all our giving to be joyful.

Joy is not just something inward, it needs to be expressed. Many of us tithe our incomes on a monthly basis and put our money into the offering once in four weeks. This means that on three Sundays we can greet others' giving with great enthusiasm and go "over the top" when it is our turn to give to God!

In the past we may have thought that if we faithfully gave God a tenth of our income, we would be expressing Kingdom lifestyle. But the Kingdom of God is not righteousness, peace and tithing! If we give a tenth without joy in the Holy Spirit we are falling short of the ideal. Only cheerful giving reflects Kingdom lifestyle.

I have used the example of money to demonstrate Kingdom living. But righteousness, peace and joy need to be expressed in all we do – at home, at school, in our work, in our Christian service...

So one way in which you can know if you are living the Kingdom lifestyle is to ask yourself the question, "Am I moving in righteousness, peace and joy in every area of my life?" If you discover that in some areas you are not, face them, pray about them and by God's grace, act on them.

Note down areas in your life where you feel you are not living the Kingdom lifestyle.

Righteousness (e.g. stealing office equipment)

....

....

....

Peace (e.g. tendency to panic when under pressure)

....

....

....

Joy (e.g. complaining when things go wrong)

....

....

....

What are your solutions to these?

Righteousness

....

....

....

Peace

....

....

....

Joy

....

....

....

Chapter 10 NOT TALK BUT POWER

In Chapter 7, I referred to two scriptures which state specifically what the Kingdom is. The first of these, as we have already seen, is found in Romans 14:17 and speaks of righteousness, peace and joy.

The second is found in 1 Corinthians 4:20.
Make sense of the verse by rearranging the letters and changing the order of the words.

tub a klat fo ratmet si ton fo het mognikd fo ropew orf dog

....

Wherever God's will is being expressed there must be evidence of divine power. The Greek word for power is "dunamis". When we first learn this, we immediately think, "Ah! That's where we get our word dynamite!" Certainly there is an obvious link between the two words, but we must not allow this to govern our thinking. In the Bible, "dunamis" had nothing to do with dynamite because when the Bible was written, dynamite had not been invented!

In the New Testament, power is nothing to do with explosions and noise. It is about the ability to preserve or transform. Christians often tend to talk a lot yet never see things changed, and it was this charge that Paul was levelling against the Corinthians. While they were busy criticizing his ministry, he was actively proclaiming the gospel in power. They saw nothing changed; he witnessed the mighty moving of God.

Christians love to tell one another what should happen in the church. "This should be changed . . . ," we say. "Why on earth have the elders decided to do that? I would have . . ." By engaging in this sort of conversation, we are in danger of imitating the Corinthians and of adopting a worldly lifestyle.

Read Acts 17:21.

How did the Athenians spend their time?

....

....

....

We must remember that the Kingdom of God is not talk but power and that we are called to live a Kingdom lifestyle.

Kingdom People Effect Change

We have already seen how the lifestyle of the Kingdom really does affect every area of our life.

I have been very challenged by a quote by H.A. Snyder who said:

"The book of Revelation graphically climaxes the theme of the new heaven and earth. God's people have been made 'a Kingdom and priests to serve our God, and they will reign on the earth' (Rev 5:10). We will see a new heaven and a new earth (Rev 21:1) which will be the final, complete, glorious fulfilment of all the Biblical promises about land.

"What does this mean for God's Kingdom now? It means we are tenants on God's land for which God is concerned and for which He has a plan that involves our stewardship of the land . . .

"The New Testament says, 'Love not the world' but nowhere are we told not to love the earth! We should love the land as God does. We are to care for it, for it is the environment of the Kingdom... It will be redeemed, transformed, turned into a land of stable peace.

"What, then, is the Promised Land for Christians? Traditionally we have viewed it as heaven in a very spiritual, non-material sense. But is it not, rather, the new earth God is bringing? The Promised Land is not earth left behind, but heaven come down. Not mansions in the sky by and by but a home on earth. The heavenly city descends to earth (Rev 21:2).

"In one sense, we already live in the Promised Land. God has given us this earth to care for. Kingdom people must tend the earth – first, because God created it; second, because it is our environment, the present location of Kingdom activity; and, finally, because the earth will be transformed into the new earth – the very locale of the Kingdom!

"This is the present meaning of land for the Kingdom of God. While the Kingdom is primarily God's reign, still there is a locale of that reign, a land of the Kingdom – the place of God's dominion. And it is the whole earth."

Kingdom lifestyle is not talk but power. People often *discuss* the state of the environment. God is looking to Christians to be zealous about *changing* it.

Some of the members of the environmental group Greenpeace have such a burden to preserve the environment that they will take drastic measures to draw attention to their cause. Several of them are prepared to lay down their lives by doing such things as jumping off boats in front of huge ships which are dumping nuclear waste. They do not spend all their time talking about change, they are acting on their beliefs.

God will redeem the earth when the Kingdom comes in its fullness. In the meantime, we should be looking after the earth, because the Kingdom is finding expression on the earth now. We have the power to change our environment and need to use it.

Our faith in God is stirred by the world around us. It has grandeur, beauty, colour and variety. In recent years, men have dived deeper in the oceans than ever before and have found hidden there the most fantastic creatures. If the fallen world is as magnificent as this, it is difficult to imagine how glorious everything will be when the Kingdom comes in its fullness.

Read Psalm 104.

Choose six aspects which reflect the wonder of God's creation and note them down.

1. ....

2. ....

3. ....

4. ....

5. ....

6. ....

Kingdom people do not just talk about the environment. They effect change in it. I should like to suggest some ways in which we could do this.

Resist waste

Many Christians live in a consumer society which quickly throws things away. We need to consider whether this is Kingdom lifestyle or whether we should resist waste.

How do you think Christians could resist waste?

....

....

....

....

....

....

Seek justice in housing

As Kingdom people who are considering the environment, we need to respond to the housing situations in the church and in society. Some members of our local church are probably living in fairly comfortable homes while others are forced by their circumstances to stay in squalid bedsits with excessively high rents. We must address this problem within the family and then consider the housing needs of people in our town.

How do you think your local church could help its poorer members?

....

....

....

....

....

....

Resist exploitation of the environment

Read Genesis 2:15.

What was Adam instructed to do?

....

....

We may be tempted to think that before the Fall there was no gardening for man to do. But this is not so – as the above scripture reveals. Clearly there was something about the earth which needed tending.

Those who are trying to live a Kingdom lifestyle must take up the challenge to care for the environment in a way that expresses the will of God.

How do you think we could do this?

....

....

....

....

....

....

So the Kingdom of God is not about rules and regulations, laws and traditions. It is righteousness, peace and joy in the Holy Spirit. It is not a life full of talk about how things should change. It is about power – the ability to see things transformed. We are called to be a people through whom God will expresses His rule and will, who demonstrate the lifestyle of the Kingdom of God.

Chapter 11 THE KINGDOM AND THE CHURCH

We have already noted that the United Kingdom is not strictly a kingdom at all. A kingdom is governed by one individual who is not voted into or out of office because he inherits his position. Since he has absolute authority, no one can challenge or oppose his decisions. His subjects live to express his will.

Christians love to proclaim the rule of God and often sing rousing songs about God's reign or Jesus' Lordship. The trouble is that although we enjoy *declaring* God's authority over us, we are sometimes reluctant to live according to His will.

Nationally, we have no experience of a kingdom. When election time comes, we vote for the government that is going to do most for us, not the one that we might most like to serve. Sadly, this "United Kingdom" thinking sometimes spills over into our understanding of the Kingdom of God.

I once spoke to a young man who seemed interested in becoming a Christian. As the conversation progressed I realized that the man's primary concern was not how he could give his life to serve God, but how God would pay his gas bill. It's true that God does provide miraculously – many of us have amazing testimonies to that effect. But here was an illustration of someone who wanted a king who would serve his subjects rather than the other way round.

Every kingdom has a sovereign and subjects. God is our sovereign and we, the church, are His people. Our goal is to obey, and live for, the King.

After Jesus had fed the five thousand, what did the people who saw the miraculous sign want to do?

.... (John 6:15)

We might wonder why Jesus refused to comply with their wishes. Why did He withdraw from them? Because He recognized that they were looking for a king who would serve them, and that was not the sort of Kingdom that He was planning to establish. So He refused to be the sort of king they wanted – one who was constantly at their beck and call. Instead, they would be His subjects – a people who would express His rule.

If I asked you, "Would you like to live in a kingdom?" my guess is that you would say, "No. I'd feel safer with a democratic, elected system of government." But on deeper reflection, you might add, "Well, it would depend on the king."

A bad ruler will look after himself and will run his nation selfishly. He will exploit his subjects and keep them poor, while he lines his own coffers and lives in luxury.

Several years ago, Brighton received a visit from the king of a North African country. He was an absolute head of state and arrived with his own bodyguard and his own bed. He stayed in the best hotel in the town and had his bedroom fitted out with mirrors. How long did he stay? One night. How much was his bill? £50,000. Bad rulers cost their subjects very dearly.

Write down the names of some twentieth-century rulers who have been exposed as bad.

....

....

....

While there are bad kings, there are also good ones. A good king will be concerned about his subjects, and his people will respond positively towards the idea of living under his rule.

Cross out in the text below the two words which are wrong and note down the correct words underneath:

"For my yoke is demanding and my burden is heavy."

.... (Matt 11:30)

Jesus is saying, "I am a good King." When we live for the Kingdom of God we are living under the rule of the best possible King.

At this point, we are not discussing the Kingdom of God in terms of church structures. We are considering the church as the King's subjects who are intent on obeying Him. As God's people live out His will, the world will see the rule of God.

A Church with Jesus' Nature and Character

If we say that the church expresses the will of God, we need to understand what that means. There are two Greek words translated as "will". One of them refers to God's eternal and absolute will, which cannot be frustrated. For example:

Look up John 6:39.

What is God's absolute will?

....

....

Will this happen?   YES/NO

The other word parallels our words "wish" and "desire". It tells us what God would like but which will not necessarily happen. For example:

Look up 2 Peter 3:9b.

What is God's desire?

....

....

Will this happen?   YES/NO

We need to pray, "Your will be done", because God's purposes can be thwarted and we want to be a people who do His will.

The Old Testament records the story of some men who were very sensitive to the will of their ruler. David, who had been anointed king by Samuel, longed for some water from the well in Bethlehem which, at that time, was behind enemy lines. He did not say to his soldiers, "You must get me some water. This is my absolute will." He was simply saying, "How wonderful it would be to have a drink from that well!" But this casual comment was sufficient to motivate three of his men to break through Philistine lines and fetch the water he wanted so much. They were sensitive to the will of their king and risked their lives to please him (1 Chron 11:15-19).

Jesus wants His church not only to have His nature but to express His character as well. When we are converted we do not receive an additional nature, but we are given a brand new one to replace the old. We are new creations, born again by the Spirit and made perfect in Christ for ever. Since we now have new natures, we *want* to do the will of God, yet sometimes lack the *ability*. This apparent inadequacy has to do with our character. By constantly working on our character, God helps us to do His will.

The will of God is like a straight line which never varies. Only one man has ever lived His life in parallel with that line – Jesus. He perfectly accomplished the will of God.

Read John 6:38.

What didn't Jesus come to do?

....

What did He come to do?

....

Fill in the gaps from Luke 22:42:

"Father, if you are .... , take this cup from me;

yet not .... , but .... be done."
This verse must be handled carefully. What is Jesus' nature? According to Philippians 2:6, He is in very nature God. This means that Jesus both wanted to do, and always could do, God's will. But as a man, He also had flesh and blood and there were times when He recoiled from His Father's will. This was the case in Gethsemane when Jesus was facing the agony and shame of the cross. He still had the ability to do God's will, but He shrank from it. His character remained completely godly because He chose the Father's will above His own.

Christ-like Character and Suffering
It is a hard lesson – that Christlike character is not produced without suffering. We are usually prepared to follow the straight line of God's will until our flesh wants to do something else. Then we stray from God's purposes and He has to bring us back on course.

Our progress in the Christian life will be as Christlike as our ability to do God's will and this will involve some suffering. At this point I am not talking about persecution for being a Christian. I am referring to the pain that you, a new creation with a new nature, will experience when you have to say "No" to your fleshly desires, which want you to do something other than God's will.

Read 1 Peter 4:1-2.

What attitude must we adopt?

....

Why?

....

The result is that we do not live the rest of this earthly life for – what?

....

but for – what?

....

To illustrate this conflict between the new nature and the desires of the flesh, let's take the area of Christian service. In the church we are sometimes in danger of becoming ministry-conscious rather than God-centred. A number of individuals are desperate to be in full-time ministry when God is actually telling them, "You need to learn how to relate to me." They go around doing many good things but they suffer because they refuse to hear God saying, "I have not called you to do that."

Even Jesus did not minister to every need. He went only where the Father told Him to go and did only what the Father said. He could have healed many people at the pool of Bethesda, but He singled out only one. Why? Because He was not ministry-conscious – trying to meet every need, without first consulting the Father and doing only as He directed.

If all the members of church are anxious to minister when they should be learning how to relate to God, then there will be pain. There will be a clash between the members' new nature, the desire to do God's will, and their own fleshly longings. They will suffer because God will work to bring them back in parallel with His will and under His rule.

Read Acts 14:21-22.

What did Paul and Barnabas say to the disciples?

"We ....

.... "

Some people say casually, "This means that you have to battle your way to heaven." But if you go along with this interpretation, you end up with a doctrine of works. And if you don't happen to meet many hardships, do you get into heaven?

Let's note that Paul and Barnabas are addressing people who are already disciples. Since our working definition of the Kingdom of God is "God's will being expressed", then what they are actually saying is this:

"We will go through many hardships if we are really going to express the rule of God, because sometimes He will have to pull us back into alignment with His will and that can be painful."

God is not simply looking for a body of people who will be with Him in glory. He is also intent on having a body of people who will demonstrate His rule on earth.

Read Revelation 5:9-10.

What does God make his people?

....

What will they do?

....

Will we see Ananias and Sapphira in heaven? I believe so. Acts 5:1-22 seems to suggest that they were believers with a new nature who wanted to do the will of God and therefore brought money to the apostles. The problem was that there was a flaw in their characters. They lied, and lying is not in the will of God so He took them straight to heaven. Through this startling act, the early church learnt that God would deal with character faults which cut across His will.

Are you going through a rough time at the moment? Then consider the possible reason for this. God wants you to be a Kingdom person who will express nothing less than His rule.

71

Chapter 12 THE RULE AND WILL OF GOD – IN GENERAL

What is the general will of God for His church?

Look up the answer in Mark 12:30-31 and write it down:

....

....

...................................,..

....

God's people express His will through every part of their being. This was
true of the Israelite nation in the Old Testament; it is also true for His
church today. God's will is, and always has been – what?

.... (Rom 12:2)

When we do the will of God, we experience His blessing. God wants to
bring the whole church into alignment with His will so that we live the
lifestyle of the Kingdom.

Some people say, ''I understand the principle – love God with all your
heart, soul, mind and strength and your neighbour as yourself – but tell me
precisely how can I do that?'' Behind this question can lie a mixture of
genuine and devious motivation. It is genuine in that the believer, with his
new nature, really wants to do the will of God. But it is devious in that this
same believer has a flesh that demands detail which he can use to his own
advantage.

So, for example, if someone is intending to talk maliciously about
another believer, he might think to himself, ''God doesn't want me to do
that because it's not His will.'' That is where the matter should end. The
problem is that his flesh wants to criticize, so he seeks to justify his
intention to gossip by adding details like, ''Everyone's got to have the

opportunity to share needs for prayer. I've been really hurt and I know I've simply got to speak out my feelings. Besides, the church encourages openness, doesn't it?'' So he gossips, and sins because he has used details to sidestep the will of God.

Howard Snyder, in his book *Kingdom Manifesto,* challenges the church to live like people who belong to the Kingdom, to get on with the job of expressing the will of God. He writes:

> ''The church is the primary point of entry into the new order of the Kingdom into present history. It is salt and light, a city on a hill. It is not the Kingdom and at times may actually betray the Kingdom, but is nevertheless in a fundamental way the sacrament and the sign of the Kingdom in today's world.
>
> "Here is both the church's high calling and her constant challenge and possibility. Yet how frequently believers misunderstand and underexperience the church as Kingdom community.
>
> "The church is called to be both redemptively present in the world and yet separated from bondage to the world's values. Here we can learn from the sixteenth century Anabaptists. As Harold Bender notes, these radical reformers gave witness to committed community and personal integrity for several basic reasons:
>
> ''(1) They insisted first of all upon personal conviction, conversion, and commitment as adults based upon prior teaching. (2) They made the above a requirement for admission to church membership. (3) They worshipped, mostly in small groups with intimacy of personal acquaintance, testimony, observation and admonition. (4) They practised church discipline. (5) They had high standards for the Christian life, which were so much higher than the average for the society of the time that only really committed persons would accept them and seek to fulfil them. (6) They practised separation from the world and so were delivered from the constant influence of the low-living multitude.''

This company of believers were different from the people around them. They stood out because they were seeking first the Kingdom.

At this point, we might be expected to consider the teaching in the Sermon on the Mount, but this would fill another book! So we shall look instead at a passage which is probably the best summary in the New Testament concerning the way that the church can express the Kingdom.

Colossians 3 first addresses the church community, then it draws more specific attention to the character of its members and gives them principles for holy living. Here we are looking at the general rule of God in the church, and in Chapter 13 we shall consider in greater detail His rule in the lives of individual believers.

Correct the following from memory:

One day you will be raised with Christ, but for now, set your affections on things on earth, where Christ is seated on the footstool of God. Set your desires on things on earth, not on heavenly things. For you are alive, and your old nature will soon be exposed by Christ to God.

Now look up Colossians 3:1-3 and write it out in separate verses.

v.1 ....

....

....

....

....

v.2 ....

....

v.3 ....

....

....

The Bible never tells us how the church should behave without first reminding us what we are. If you look at the first part of Colossians 3:1, you will see that it informs us that every member of the church has been raised with Christ. We demonstrate that we have a new nature by going through baptism in water.

Fill in the gaps from Col 2:12:

. . . having been .... with him in ....

and .... with him through ....

in the .... of God, who .... Him

from the ....

Christian baptism celebrates resurrection. We do not take into the baptistry the words of Esther, "If I perish, I perish"!

It is vitally important to the apostle Paul that Christians understand what has happened to them. "You died," he says. "And your life is now hidden with Christ in God." We are absolutely secure.

Write out Colossians 3:4 and, if you are a Christian, change the word "your" to "my" and "you" to "I":

....

....

....

Whenever I read this verse I picture a splendid royal procession. On occasions the Queen comes out for an opening of parliament, or some other great state event. Excited crowds line the pavements waiting for her to appear. When she emerges in her open carriage, she is in the centre of a huge company of people. The band strikes up a rousing march, and as she passes by, all the onlookers wave flags and cheer.

Christians are waiting for a royal event which will outshine all others in history. When King Jesus returns for His Kingdom, He will come in a magnificent procession. On that day, you will not be an onlooker, another face in the crowds. You will appear with Him in glory.

Read 1 John 3:2.

What are you now?

....

What will you be when Jesus appears?

....

Exciting, isn't it?!

Chapter 13 THE RULE AND WILL OF GOD – IN DETAIL

After Paul has reminded us that we are new creations in Christ, he goes on to deal with our character. How, in *detail* rather than in general principle, can our characters be conformed to the will of God? How can we keep to the parallel line and be the sort of people who consistently express the Kingdom, the rule of God?

Paul tells us that there are things that we must put off and other things that we must put on.

Put Off . . .

Colossians 3:5 says: "Put to death, therefore, whatever belongs to your earthly nature." This translation is unfortunate since it implies that we have two natures, one old and the other new. I have already refuted this idea from the scriptures.

Your nature is "the essential you". If you are an unbeliever, then that nature is old and if you are a believer, that nature is new. The problem is that Christians live in bodies of flesh which, as we have seen, make them wander away from God's will. The literal translation of the word which the New International Version translates "earthly nature" is "earthly members". So your earthly members, not your essential new nature, cause you to stray from the straight line of God's will and into forbidden territory.

According to Colossians 3:5 what specific things must we put off?

....

....

....

These things are predominantly sexual sins, the sort of sins which we are perhaps most tempted to commit. The world encourages us to believe that faithfulness to one partner for life is not appropriate in our day and age.

Sexual satisfaction outside marriage may be called acceptable in the world but it is called sin in the Kingdom.

I have great reservations about the interest which believers express in some "soap operas" on television. They may not be visually sexually explicit, but they are dangerous because they subtly feed our minds and tempt our members to submit to worldly values.

To retain our purity we need high motivation. We have it – because we are new creations who have been raised with Christ. God does not want us to be a people who are constantly wandering into and out of sin. He wants to be King over a distinctive company who will express His will and reflect the glory of His own perfect character.

Read Colossians 3:6.

What is coming as a result of the evils mentioned in verse 5?

....

In verse 7 Paul reminds us that although we used to do these things, we must not do them any more. Why? Because Kingdom people have a new nature and must therefore display a radically different lifestyle from the world – in their sexual expression, and also in other things.

According to Colossians 3:8-9a what other specific things must we put off?

....

....

....

The words that you have just written are commonly expressed through the lips. God wants a people who will demonstrate His rule by the way that they speak. Sometimes we forget this. In fact, the church is very prone to gossip, three of the most fascinating words in the English language being, "Have you heard...?" But citizens of heaven do not talk spitefully about others. If we are truly seeking first the Kingdom, then we must tame our tongues.

If our speech is sound, what can we do? Read James 3:20.

....

78

To encourage people to speak righteously, I often use the acronym, "THINK". Before you speak, ask yourself:

Is this . . .

        True?

        Helpful (even if it is true)?

        Inconsistent (with my new nature)?

        Necessary (is it going to edify)?

        Kind?

If we are going to be a distinctive community of God's people, we must think before we speak.

Think for a moment. Have you said anything recently that you regret? If so, seek God's forgiveness now and, if necessary, apologize to the person concerned.

Having exhorted us to speak well, Paul is at pains to remind us of our position in Christ and to underline that He is after our character.

Fill in the gaps from Col 3:9b-10:

. . .you have .... your .... with

its .... and have .... the

.... , which is being .... in ....

in the .... of its ....

In Colossians 3:3 the apostle says, "You died," and in verse 5 he encourages us to "put to death" earthly things. We have died and been raised with Christ so we have a new nature. The flesh, however, is far from perfect. We lack the ability to change, so God helps us by transforming us steadily into the image of His Son and aligning our character with His will. We are in the process of change.

Paul tells us that where people are expressing the will of God, the barriers go down. In Colossians 3:11 he says that there is . . .

no Greek or Jew	– no racial barrier
no circumcised or uncircumcised	– no ceremonial barrier
no barbarian	– no cultural barrier
no Scythian	– no social barrier
no slave or free	– no status barrier

The barbarians were so called because they seemed to communicate in words that sounded like ba, ba, ba. The Scythians were regarded as the lowest group among the barbarians. Someone said of them, "They had the most filthy habits and never washed with water. They delighted in murdering people and were little better than wild beasts."

But in Christ all the barriers go down because the grace of God bridges all chasms. "Christ is all" (that matters) and He is "in all" – in the Greek, the Jew, the circumcised, the uncircumcised, the barbarian, the Scythian, the slave, the free, the English, the Scotsman, the American . . . He is in all who believe. We are one people, the Kingdom community for whom togetherness is a Kingdom characteristic. Let us make sure that we put off anything that might hinder our unity as the people of the King.

Is God asking you to "put off" anything? If so, write it down here.

....

....

....

Put On . . .

Christians must not stay with the negative, we must move on to the positive. We are "God's chosen people, holy and dearly loved" (Col 3:12a). These are covenant terms which remind us that we have been set apart for God. As His community we must express His rule by replacing bad things with good ones.

According to Colossians 3:12b what five specific things must we put on?

1. .... 2. ....

3. .... 4. .... 5. ....

Since we have a new nature, we are able to put these things on. It is a bit like looking in a wardrobe and selecting something to wear. We must assign the old clothes to the dustbin and choose garments which are appropriate for Kingdom people to wear.

Fill in the gaps from Col 3:13-14:

.... each other and forgive ....

grievances you may have against one another. Forgive .... the

Lord forgave you. And over all these virtues put on .... ,

which .... them all ....

in ....

At times, Christians will fail one another but there is never any excuse for
unforgivingness and lack of love. You may argue, ''I've been wronged!
He's hurt me so much! I can't forgive him!'' But you can, and the reason
is this: Christ has forgiven you. As a new person you can put on
forgiveness and love, and maintain Kingdom unity.

Without reference to the scriptures, rearrange the following words to
quote Colossians 3:15, then check your answer:

since you were called as thankful members of one Christ, in peace. let
the body rule to your hearts of peace.

....

....

....

Alongside righteousness and joy, peace is a characteristic of the Kingdom
and therefore of the church. How do we put on peace? We do as the verse
says. Rather than criticize other members of the church, we express
thankfulness for them. Then peace will rule among us.

According to Colossians 3:16a, how should we let the word of Christ
dwell in us?

....

Sadly, we sometimes let the word of Christ dwell in us, but not to the
degree that Paul exhorts us. ''Yes, I agree with tithing,'' we say. ''Now
does that mean gross or net? It probably means net, so I've got to give
£5.92 a week. The car journey here costs about 42p, so I'm left with £5.50.
To make it easier, I'll put £5.00 in the plate.'' Here, the word of God dwells
in you, but not richly.

Fill in the gaps from Col 3:16b:

... teach and .... one another with all .... ,

and as you .... , ... and ....

.... with .... in your ....to

....

The translation of this verse is not very accurate. It should be, "Teach and admonish one another through what you sing." When we worship together, we are not only exalting God but proclaiming the truth to one another as well. The same principle is seen elsewhere in scripture.

Look up Ephesians 5:19.

How are we encouraged to communicate with each other?

through ....

How are we encouraged to communicate with God?

by ....

Add the two missing words:

And .... you do, whether in word of deed, do it .... in the name of the Lord Jesus, giving thanks to God the Father through him (Col 3:17).

We express the will of God when we live to please Him in everything – through our words, actions and attitudes.

What is God asking you to "put on"?

....

....

....

Conclusion

The clock in the exam room indicated to Jim that he had only five more minutes to work on the Kingdom question. "I'll just make sure I've included everything," he thought. "Then I'll write a final paragraph." Glancing through his rough outline, he read:

What is the Kingdom of God?
It's the government of God – His rule and authority on earth.
It's "God's will being expressed".

How can we seek it first?
Through words, works and wonders
Through righteousness, peace and joy
Not through talk but through power

We express Kingdom lifestyle in the church by living:

  righteously:
- having our sexual appetites under control
- speaking well of others
- ensuring that no barriers disrupt our unity in Christ

  peacefully:
- letting the peace of Christ rule in our hearts

  joyfully:
- being thankful for others
- expressing joy in songs of gratitude to God.

Jim nodded approvingly, then he picked up his pen and wrote the final paragraph:

Jesus taught us to pray, "Your Kingdom come, your will be done on earth as it is in heaven". The Kingdom of God is God's rule and authority. How do you recognize the people who are truly seeking first the Kingdom? You look for the hallmarks. Their lives express God's will. They are righteous, peaceful and joyful, and at every opportunity they proclaim the gospel with words, works and wonders. When you see the marks of the Kingdom, then you know that the Kingdom has come.

Jim chewed the end of his biro again and gazed out of the window at the activity in the street below. "Amazing idea!" he thought. "God's glorious Kingdom established on earth through His people! I wonder how many Christians realize that God is relying on them to bring in His Kingdom."

Then, turning back to his exam paper, he began the next question.

FOR YOUR NOTES

FOR YOUR NOTES

More titles in the

How to...

S T U D Y   S E R I E S

Praying The Lord's Prayer

is a practical workbook for those who want to maintain a consistent and effective prayer life, and can be used by individuals or groups. Taking Jesus' prayer structure as a model, it develops the themes of the fatherhood and names of God, the nature of God's will, reign and kingdom and His gifts and forgiveness in our lives.

Terry Virgo is based at Clarendon Church, Brighton. He also leads the *New Frontiers* team committed to planting and serving churches in the UK and overseas. He is author of *Restoration in the Church* and *Men of Destiny*.

Catalogue Number YB 9177   £1.70

Handling Your Money

is a Bible-based workbook on managing your personal finances. Beginning with the idea of God as giver, the book discusses our attitudes towards wealth, money and possessions. It contains advice on budgeting and avoiding debt, and teaches us how to be abundant givers ourselves. This workbook is suitable for both individual and group use.

John Houghton leads the eldership team at Hailsham Christian Fellowship, Sussex. His wider ministry as a speaker and writer reflects his concern for Christians to face the practical, social and moral implications of the gospel in today's world. John and his wife Janet have three teenage children. His previous books are *Hagbane's Doom, Gublak's Greed* and *Surin's Revenge* (for children), *The Healthy Alternative* and *A Touch of Love.*

Catalogue Number 9176   £1.70

Learning to Worship

is a devotional workbook for use by both individuals and groups who want, in the author's words, to 'appreciate from the Scriptures this magnificent gem that God has so graciously allowed us to rediscover'. Whether we are worshipping alone or among God's people, this book offers Scriptural insights to help us become the worshippers that God is seeking.

Phil Rogers is the Senior Pastor of New Life Christian Church, South Lee. He is a keyboard player and compiles the yearly songbook for the Downs Bible Week. His own songs include *Who is This?* and *How precious, O Lord.* He is also involved in teaching and training worship leaders. Phil lives in South East London with his wife Sandy and their three sons.

Catalogue Number YB 9179

£1.80

Effective Evangelism

is a workbook for individuals, groups and church leaders. Beginning with the Biblical teaching on evangelism, it goes on to give practical advice on making contact with non-Christians, giving a testimony, planning a guest service and so on.

Ben Davies is the senior minister of Bracknell Baptist Church, Berkshire. In 1964 the church numbered about 20 people, and today has a congregation of over 500, with 6 full-time staff. Ben also gives pastoral advice to a number of other churches as a member of the *New Frontiers* team. He is a Welshman, and he and his wife Maureen have three teenage children.

Catalogue Number YB 9175 £1.70